The La[illegible]
For the Truth

(based on ahadith from
Bukhari, Muslim and Abu Dawud)

by
Abdassamad Clarke

Ta-Ha Publishers
1 Wynne Road
London SW9 0BB
UK

Published
Rajab 1421/October 2000 by:

Ta-Ha Publishers Ltd.
1 Wynne Road
London SW9 0BB
website: http://www.taha.co.uk
email: sales@taha.co.uk

By: Abdassamad Clarke
General Editor: Afsar Siddiqui

A catalogue record for this book is available from the British Library.

ISBN 1 897940 95 5

Typeset by: Bookwright
website: http://www.bogvaerker.dk/Bookwright
email: Bookwright@bogvaerker.dk

Printed and bound by: Deluxe Printers, London.
email: de-luxe@Talk21.com

Contents

بسم الله الرحمن الرحيم

Introduction

Some people tell history as if it is only battles, kings and empires. Such people look at Islam and call it something like, "The Islamic Empire" or even worse, "The Arabic Empire". This story is not just one of armies, empires and battles. So, as we tell the story of the great expedition of Tabuk against the eastern half of the Roman Empire, we will tell the story of one man among the Muslims at that time: Ka'b ibn Malik, may Allah be pleased with him.

A number of people stayed behind from the expedition to Tabuk. Some of them were hypocrites who had no real excuse, but three of them were Muslims who had become distracted by their new wealth and property and had just not gone.

One of them was Ka'b ibn Malik, who was one of the two great poets among the Companions. When he was old, he became blind and his son 'Abdullah used to guide him around. He told 'Abdullah his own story.

Ka'b's story in his own words

I did not stay at home during any battle that the Messenger of Allah fought except the battle of Tabuk.

I had not taken part in the battle of Badr. But Allah did not blame anyone who had not participated in it, because the Messenger of Allah had gone out in search of Quraysh's caravan (he had not gone out for battle). Allah made the Muslims and their enemy meet without any appointment for battle.

I was present at the night of al-'Aqabah before the Hijrah with the Messenger of Allah when we pledged for Islam. I would not exchange it for the battle of Badr although the battle of Badr is more famous among people.

As for what happened to me in this battle of Tabuk, I had never been stronger or wealthier than I was when I stayed at home during that battle of the Prophet. By Allah, I had never had two she-camels before, but I did at the time of this battle.

Whenever the Messenger of Allah wanted to make an expedition, he used to hide his intention by apparently referring to a different expedition.

At the time of the expedition to Tabuk, which the Messenger of Allah went on in severe heat, facing a long journey, the desert, and a great number of enemies, he told the Muslims clearly where they were going so that they would be prepared for the expedition.

The Messenger of Allah, peace be upon him, was accompanied by so many Muslims that a record could not be kept. Any man who intended to stay away would have thought that his absence would remain hidden, unless Allah revealed it through Divine Revelation.

The Messenger of Allah went on that expedition at the time when the fruits had ripened and the shade was pleasant.

* * *

But as usual we have gone ahead of our story. We will come back to Ka'b and his story later. Let us go back to the Opening of Makkah. The kafirun are those who cover over the truth. They call this the *Conquest* of Makkah, but this is not the right name, since there was no battle and little fighting. In Arabic the word used, *Fath*, means 'Opening'. At this event, Makkah *opened* to Islam.

The Opening of Makkah

The story begins after the Opening of Makkah in 9 AH/630 CE when the people of Makkah accepted Islam. All the Arabs respected Quraysh because they were the descendants of Isma'il and Ibrahim, peace be upon both of them. The Arabs had only been waiting and watching to see what Quraysh would do about this new thing, Islam. When Quraysh accepted it, most other people raced to become Muslims. It looked as if the whole story of Islam was coming to a wonderful conclusion. Who could have imagined that all the Arabs would be united in Islam?

Then as now, the Arabs were the single most difficult people in the world to unite. They had no kings or empires, many of them travelled in the deserts alone except for their families. They had no education or philosophy, no organised religion such as Judaism or Christianity. Those who followed the Way of Ibrahim, peace be upon him, were people of *fitrah*: they lived and worshipped Allah naturally. Thus, the Arabs' accepting Islam as an entire race of people was astonishing. Some people thought that perhaps this was as far as Islam would go, and that it was enough.

However, the Prophet, peace be upon him, had written letters to various foreign rulers. He wrote to the Emperor of the Persians, and to Heraclius the ruler of the Byzantine Christians. Let us look at the Byzantines and their Christianity.

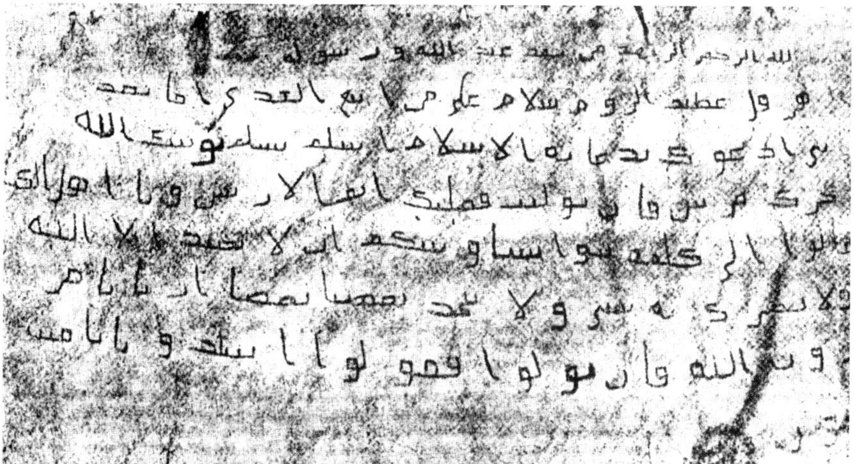

Original of Prophet's Letter to Emperor Heraclius

The Christians and the Romans

'Isa, peace be upon him, lived without the things of the world. The early Christians who followed him were poor and were not strong in the world. The Roman Empire persecuted them mercilessly. Nevertheless, Christianity spread. The people who became Christians fastest were the slaves and the poorest of the people.

The Empire was built on slavery and the slaves' lives were very hard. Unfortunately, they were only told about the kind of Christianity which we know is false. They were told the lie that 'Isa, peace be upon him, was crucified, that he suffered terribly, died, was laid in a sepulchre, and then after three days rose again. This was the terrible story that the slaves were told.

Because the slaves' own lives were so difficult they were greatly moved by this awful story. They liked the thought that a man who suffered and was killed, would really rise from the dead and be someone very important on the Last Day. They liked the thought that all the weak and poor people would have revenge on the rich and powerful people.

So this falsehood spread very quickly among the slaves in the Roman Empire. This rapid spread even made the Empire unstable.

However, there were still many true Christians. They did not believe that Jesus was a god, or a part of god. These groups and many others argued with each other a lot. The arguments were so serious that the Empire itself was in danger of losing its unity. If that happened, it would have been in danger from its enemies.

The emperor at that time was Constantine the Great. He was not a Christian, but he assembled the Christians to resolve the debate. This was the Council of Nicaea and it happened in 325 CE. However, although the Council decided in favour of the false trinitarian Christianity, it didn't really solve any problems. The two sides were still at loggerheads. Constantine later began to lean towards the unitarians who did not believe that 'Isa, peace be upon him, was a god. He is even said to have died as a unitarian.

The trinitarians worked away at getting power over the Empire, until finally the official religion of the Roman Empire became trinitarian Christianity. They believed that there were three gods which were really one god! Now you can see why it was not the

Romans who gave the world good arithmetic! If they started with three which are at the same time one, then they were obviously hopeless at sums.

However, at the same time as the Christians took control of the Roman Empire, the Empire took control of Christianity. There is nothing better for an empire than a good religion. It unifies people because they believe that they are fighting for a god or even 'the' god. It is much easier to collect taxes, and taxes in the Roman Empire were quite heavy. Maybe they were not as heavy as today but they were high by any standards.

Under Diocletian, the Empire had split into the Western Empire and the Eastern Empire, but Constantine reunited it briefly. He rebuilt the old Greek city Byzantium, called it Constantinople and made it his capital. Later, the Goths sacked Rome itself in 410 CE so the Western Empire was destroyed. However, the Eastern Empire remained, and it is sometimes called the Byzantine Empire because the old name of Constantinople was Byzantium.

Although Constantinople was in Greece it was the centre of the Eastern 'Roman' Empire. Its language and culture were Greek. This can lead to a confusion, because in Arabic these people are called *ar-Rum*, so sometimes they are called 'the Romans', but sometimes 'the Greeks'. Now you can see why there is some truth in both.

All of this takes us up to just before the beginning of our story. The Byzantine Empire was Christian, but they persecuted all the other types of Christians, including those who really followed the revelation given to 'Isa, peace be upon him. The ones who really followed him then were very few. Today, perhaps there is no one who truly follows him except the Muslims.

MAP

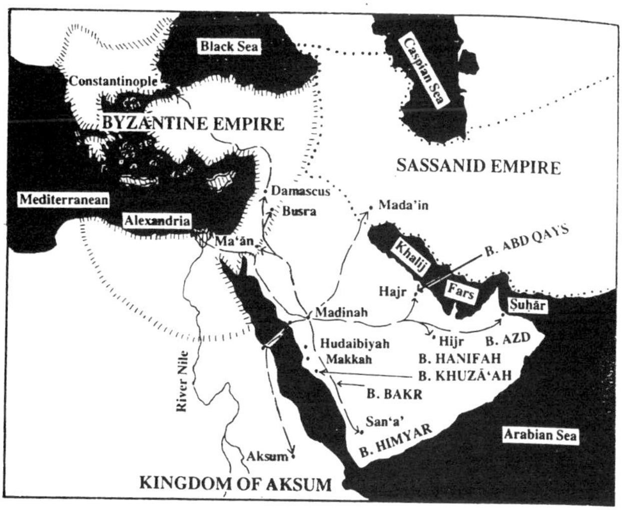

Map showing only such countries, places, areas, boundaries, cities and tribes which are relevant to the different descriptions in the monograph, e.g., in the pennisula of Arabia only names of such tribes are given with which the article deals.

Instead of drawing arrows in a straight line between Madinah and the cities where the religious letters were despatched, the arrows are drawn on the basis of traditional trade routes.

The arrows terminate either at the capitals (e.g. Aksum) or at tribal headquarters (e.g. Ṣuḥār) or at the seats of the Byzantine prefects (e.g. Ma'ān).

Boundaries of the Byzantine Empire //////////

Boundaries of the Sassanid Empire ....

Heraclius

Abu Sufyan was one of the leading men of Quraysh. He was opposed to the Prophet. He was a merchant and would often travel north into the lands which are today called Palestine and Syria, which at that time were occupied by the Byzantines.

Abu Sufyan said that while he was accompanying a caravan belonging to Quraysh on its way to do business in Sham,* Heraclius sent a messenger to him. This was at the time when the Messenger of Allah, peace be upon him, had made a truce with Abu Sufyan and the disbelievers of Quraysh (see *The Clear Victory*). This was some time before the Opening of Makkah which we mentioned earlier.

Abu Sufyan and his companions went to Heraclius who was then at Jerusalem. Heraclius summoned them to his court where all the important Romans were around him. He called for his Arabic translator.

* Sham is today divided up into Syria, Israel, Palestine, Lebanon and Jordan.

Heraclius asked them, "Who among you is closely related to that man who claims to be a Prophet?"

Abu Sufyan replied, "I am the nearest relative to him among the group."

Heraclius said, "Bring him (Abu Sufyan) close to me and make his companions stand behind him."

Abu Sufyan later said, "Heraclius told his translator to tell my companions that he wanted to ask me some questions regarding that man (the Prophet) and that if I told a lie they should contradict me." Abu Sufyan added, "By Allah! If I had not been afraid of my companions calling me a liar, I would not have spoken the truth about the Prophet."

"The first question he asked me was, 'What standing does his family have among you?' I said, 'He belongs to a good family among us.'

"Heraclius then asked, 'Has anybody among you ever claimed the same (i.e. to be a Prophet) before him?' I replied, 'No.'

"He said, 'Was anybody among his ancestors a king?' I answered, 'No.'

"Heraclius asked, 'Do nobles follow him or poor people?' I replied, 'The poor follow him.'

"He said, 'Are his followers increasing or decreasing in numbers?' I said, 'They are increasing.'

"He then asked, 'Do any of those who embrace his way become displeased and renounce the way afterwards?' I told him, 'No.'

"Heraclius said, 'Had you ever accused him of telling lies before his claim (to be a Prophet)?' I answered, 'No. '

"Heraclius said, 'Does he break his promises?' I said, 'No. We have a truce with him, but we do not know what he will do in it.' I could not find a way to say anything against him except that.

"Heraclius asked, 'Have you ever had a war with him?' I answered, 'Yes.'

"Then he said, 'What was the result of the battles?' I said, 'Sometimes he was victorious and sometimes we were.'

"Heraclius said, 'What does he tell you to do?' I answered, 'He tells us to worship Allah alone and not to worship anything along with Him, and to give up everything false that our ancestors had said. He tells us to pray, to speak the truth, to be decent and to keep good relations with our families and relations.'

"Heraclius asked the translator to tell me, 'I asked you about his family and your reply was that he belongs to a very noble family. All the Messengers come from noble families among their peoples. I asked you whether anybody else among you had ever claimed such a thing. You said no. If the answer had been yes, I would have thought that this man was following the previous man. Then I asked you whether anyone of his ancestors was a king. Your reply was no. If it had been yes, I would have thought that this man wanted to take back his ancestral kingdom. I asked whether he was ever accused of telling lies before he said what he said (that he was a prophet), and your reply was no. So I wondered how a person who does not tell a lie about other people could ever tell a lie about Allah. I then asked you whether the rich follow him or the poor. You said that it is the poor who follow him. All the Messengers have been followed by the poor. Then I asked you whether his followers are increasing or decreasing in numbers. You replied that they are increasing. This is the way of true faith, until it is complete. I asked you whether there is anybody, who, after embracing his way, became displeased and discarded his way. Your reply was no. This is (the sign of) true faith. Its delight enters the hearts and mixes with them completely. I asked you whether he had ever betrayed anyone. You said no. The Messengers never betray. Then I asked you what he tells you to do. You said that he tells you to worship Allah alone and not to worship anything along with Him. You said he tells you not to worship idols and tells you to pray, speak the

They ran towards the gates of the palace like wild animal......

truth and be decent. If what you have said is true, he will very soon occupy this place beneath my feet. I knew (from the revealed books) that he was going to appear but I did not know that he would be from you. If I could reach him, I would definitely go to meet him right away. If I were with him, I would certainly wash his feet.'"

Heraclius then asked for the letter sent to him by the Messenger of Allah. It had been delivered by a Muslim called Dihyah to the Byzantine Governor of Busra, who sent it on to Heraclius to read.

The letter was as follows:

> "In the name of Allah the Merciful, the Compassionate. From Muhammad the slave of Allah and His Messenger to Heraclius the ruler of Byzantine. Peace be upon whoever follows the guidance. I invite you to Islam. If you become a Muslim you will be safe, and Allah will double your reward. If you reject this invitation to Islam you will be doing a great wrong action by misguiding your peasants."

Then the Messenger had written the ayah of Qur'an:

> "O People of the Book! Come to a word common to you and us that we worship none but Allah and that we associate nothing in worship with Him, and that none of us will take

others as Lords beside Allah. Then, if they turn away, say: 'Bear witness that we are Muslims (those who have surrendered to Allah)'." (Qur'an, Surah Al 'Imran: 64).

Abu Sufyan added, "When Heraclius had finished his speech and had read the letter, there was a great hue and cry in the Court and we were turned out.

"I told my companions that the matter of Ibn Abi Kabsha (the Prophet Muhammad) had become so important that even the King of Bani al-Asfar (the Byzantine Romans) is afraid of him. Then I began to be sure that he (the Prophet) would be the conqueror in the near future, until later I embraced Islam."

Once Heraclius was visiting Jerusalem. He got up one morning in a sad mood. Some of his priests asked him why he was in that mood. Heraclius could sometimes foretell the future and he was an astrologer.

He replied, "Last night when I looked at the stars, I saw that the leader of those who practise circumcision had conquered (us). Who practises circumcision?"

The people said, "Only the Jews practise circumcision, but you should not be afraid of them. Just give orders to kill every Jew in the country."

While they were discussing this, a messenger was

brought in who had been sent to bring the news about the Messenger of Allah to Heraclius. Heraclius heard the news, then he told the people to go and see whether the messenger from the Arab tribe of Ghassan was circumcised. They told Heraclius that he was. Heraclius asked the messenger about the Arabs, and he said, "The Arabs also practise circumcision."

Heraclius remarked that the kingdom of the Arabs had appeared. He then wrote a letter to a friend in Rome who was as knowledgeable as him. Then Heraclius left for a town in Syria called Homs. He stayed there until he received his friend's reply. The friend agreed with him about the arrival of the Prophet and accepted that he was a Prophet.

Heraclius invited all the leading Byzantines to assemble in his palace at Homs. When they were gathered, he ordered all doors in the palace closed.

Then he came in and said, "Byzantines! If you want success and if you are looking for right guidance; if you want your empire to endure then pledge allegiance to this Prophet." He meant that they should accept Islam.

They ran towards the gates of the palace like wild animals but found the doors closed. Heraclius realised that they hated Islam. He lost hope that they would embrace Islam, so he ordered that they should be brought back.

Then he said to them, "What I said was just to test the strength of your conviction. Now I have seen it." The people prostrated before him and were pleased with him. This was the end of Heraclius' story. He died in February 641 CE. He never accepted Islam, and his armies fought against the Muslims.

Mu'tah

Then the Prophet, peace be upon him, sent the Muslim army against the Byzantines at Mu'tah. The Messenger of Allah, may Allah bless him and grant him peace, knew how huge the Byzantine army was. He put his beloved Zaid ibn Harithah in charge of the Muslim army. Zaid was the young man whom some Arabs had enslaved before Islam. Khadijah had bought him and given him to the Prophet. There was a great love between them.

The Prophet knew that Zaid might be killed, so he appointed Ja'far ibn Abi Talib, his own cousin and the brother of 'Ali, as the second man to take command if that happened. You can see the great importance of this battle, since the Messenger of Allah put two of the people of the people of whom he was most fond in charge knowing that they could be killed. Then he appointed Abdullah ibn Rawahah as the third man to take charge if the first two were both killed.

The army left for Mu'tah where they fought the

Byzantine army which was much bigger and better armed than the Muslims. Many of the Muslims were killed, including all three of the men who had been made leaders. Then Khalid ibn al-Walid took charge and saved the day.

The Year of the Deputations

The year in which our story begins, 9 AH/ 630 CE is called 'The Year of the Deputations', because, after the Conquest of Makkah, all the Arabian tribes sent representatives to Madinah to accept Islam. Those people learnt as much of Islam as they could and went back to teach their people.

Musaylimah the Liar

Also in that year, a man called Maslamah wrote a letter to the Messenger of Allah in which he claimed to be a prophet. He wrote:

"From Maslamah, the messenger of Allah, to Muhammad the Messenger of Allah. Let us divide the land between us."

The Messenger of Allah, may Allah bless him and grant him peace, wrote back:

> "From Muhammad the Messenger of Allah, to Musaylimah the Liar. The land belongs to Allah. He makes whomever He wishes inherit it."

Musaylimah means 'Little Maslamah'. He was only to stop his mischief later in the time when Abu Bakr was khalifah, may Allah be pleased with him, and he sent an army against him. Many people were killed, but Musaylimah too was killed.

The Expedition to Tabuk

The expedition to Tabuk is also known as the "Army of Difficulty".

After the Opening the Prophet, peace be upon him, wrote a letter to the tribes who had not accepted Islam. He invited them to Islam. He also wrote to those who had accepted Islam and called them to join an expedition against the Byzantines. He made an appointment to meet them at Tabuk.

News had come that the Byzantines had gathered a large army in Syria. They said that Heraclius had paid a year's salary to the troops so that they would be ready for a long struggle.

There were a number of Arab tribes who lived on the edge of the desert close to the Byzantines. They were called Lakhm, Judham, 'Amilah and Ghassan. Some of them were Christian Arabs and they had joined the Byzantines. The Prophet, may Allah bless him and grant him peace, knew that this was a threat to Islam, so he told people to get ready for an expedition.

Whenever the Messenger of Allah meant to go on an expedition, he would hide his real destination from his companions for reasons of security.

The expedition was going to take place in very hot weather. The journey would be very long and through deserted wasteland. They might meet and fight powerful enemies.

The Prophet, may Allah bless him and grant him peace, made the situation clear to the Muslims. He wanted them to prepare themselves and get ready to fight, so he told them where they were going and who they were going to fight.

It was the most difficult time of the year for such a journey.

First, it was the summer time and therefore extremely hot. It would be even hotter in the desert.

Second, it was exactly at the time of the date harvest. The people of Madinah who had date-palms should be hard at work harvesting their crops.

Third, it came at the time when the victory of Islam seemed almost total. Some people thought that the fight was over. Now here was an expedition not against a small Arab tribe, but against the mighty Byzantine Empire.

These are some of the reasons that it is known as the Army of Difficulty.

Ka'b ibn Malik, whom we met earlier, had no real excuses. He said, "The Messenger of Allah and his companions prepared for the battle. I started to get myself ready along with them, but I returned without doing anything. I would say to myself, 'I can still do that.'"

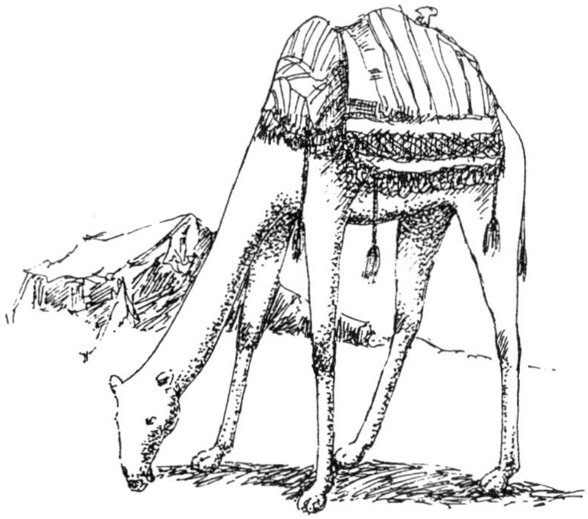

Fitting out the Army

It was a difficult time to fit out such an army. The Prophet, may Allah bless him and grant him peace, ordered the Muslims to give sadaqah for it.

Sayyiduna 'Uthman

The Messenger told people to support the Army of Difficulty. Then 'Uthman ibn 'Affan said, "Messenger of Allah, I will be responsible for supplying one hundred camels with their saddle blankets and their saddles, in the way of Allah."

Then he again urged people to support the army. 'Uthman said, "Messenger of Allah, I will be responsible for supplying two hundred camels with their saddle blankets and their saddles, in the way of Allah."

Then for a third time he urged people to support the army and 'Uthman said, "Messenger of Allah, I will be responsible for supplying three hundred camels with their saddle blankets and their saddles, in the way of Allah."

Then the Messenger of Allah, may Allah bless him and grant him peace, came down from the minbar saying, "There will be nothing at all against 'Uthman whatever he does after this."

'Uthman also brought the Prophet one thousand dinars when he equipped the Army of Difficulty. He poured them into his lap. The Messenger of Allah began turning them over, saying, "Nothing 'Uthman does after this day will harm him," twice.

The setting out and the journey

He set out for the journey on a Thursday which was his usual custom. It is said that the army was thirty thousand men with ten thousand horses.

The Prophet, may Allah bless him and grant him peace, set off at the beginning of Rajab two months before Ramadan.

But what about Ka'b? As he himself said, "I kept on delaying it. Then the people were ready. The Messenger of Allah left and the Muslims along with him. I had not prepared anything for my departure. I said to myself, 'I will get ready one or two days after him, and then join them.' In the morning after their departure, I went out to get myself ready but returned having done nothing. Then again the next morning, I went out to get ready but returned without doing anything.

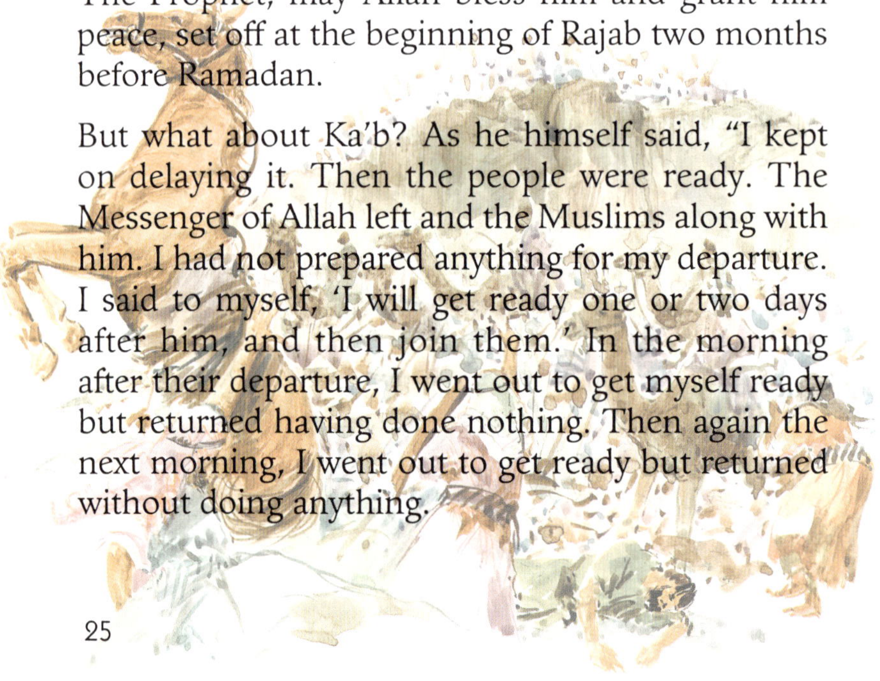

"It went on like that until they had hurried away and the battle was missed. Even then I meant to go and overtake them. I wish I had done so! But it was not to be.

"After the departure of the Messenger of Allah, whenever I went out and walked among the people who had remained behind, it made me sad. I could see no one around me, except for those accused of hypocrisy or one of those weak men whom Allah excuses."

Let us see the others who did not go on this expedition.

Some who stayed behind

A large number of the hypocrites did not come on this expedition. We will look at some of their stories later. It is said there were as many as eighty of them.

The men who wept

There were seven men who had nothing on which to ride and they came to ask the Messenger of Allah to give them riding animals so that they could come on the expedition. The Messenger, peace be upon him, had nothing on which to let them ride and so they turned away with tears in their eyes because they could not come to the battle. Allah mentioned them in the Qur'an because of that:

> And nothing is held against those who, when they came to you for you to provide them with mounts and you said, "I cannot find anything on which to mount you," turned away with their eyes overflowing with tears, overcome by grief at finding nothing to spend.

Abu Dharr

Abu Dharr and another man did not set off with the army because of some matters which held them up. Nevertheless, each of them set off by himself and travelled alone across the desert. They could not allow themselves to keep away from a battle which the Messenger and the Companions were fighting.

Al-Hijr

The community of al-Hijr – *Ashab al-Hijr* – mentioned in the Qur'an are the same people as Thamud. Al-Hijr was one of the cities founded by those people.

When Allah's Messenger, may Allah bless him and grant him peace, arrived at al-Hijr during the expedition to Tabuk, he told his companions not to drink water from its well or take away water from it. They said, "We have already kneaded the dough (to bake bread) with its water, and filled our water-bags with it." The Prophet, peace be upon him, told them to throw away the dough and pour out the water.

Thamud were a great and powerful people, not as mighty as the Byzantines, but with a similar type of empire. They thought that building great buildings and having armies and a state made them so mighty that they did not need Allah. They rejected their prophet, Salih, peace be upon him, and Allah destroyed them.

Hunger and a Miracle

During the expedition, the provisions ran short and the men suffered from extreme hunger. They said, "Messenger of Allah, will you allow us to slaughter our camels? We shall eat them and use their fat."

The Messenger of Allah, peace be upon him, said, "Do as you please."

Then 'Umar came and said, "Messenger of Allah, if you do that, we will be short of riding animals. But tell them to bring their remaining provisions, then ask for Allah's blessings on them. Perhaps Allah will bless them."

The Messenger of Allah agreed. He called for a leather mat to be used as a tablecloth and spread it out. Then he called people to bring the remains of their provisions. Some came with a handful of dates, others with portions of bread. Some small quantities of these things were collected on the tablecloth.

Then the Messenger of Allah asked for blessings

on them. He said, "Fill your vessels with these provisions."

They filled their vessels to the brim. No one among the army of 30,000 people was left with a single empty vessel. They ate their fill, and there was still some left over.

The Messenger of Allah, may Allah bless him and grant him peace, said, "I bear witness that there is no god but Allah and I am the Messenger of Allah. Whoever meets his Lord not doubting these two truths will not be kept out of the Garden."

Joining prayers

On the journey the Prophet, peace be upon him, and the Companions shortened the prayers and joined them together. Mu'adh ibn Jabal, may Allah be pleased with him, said, "We set out with the Messenger of Allah on the expedition to Tabuk. He prayed the noon and afternoon prayers together, and the sunset and night prayers together."

Mu'adh also said, "On the expedition to Tabuk if the sun had passed the midpoint of the sky before the Apostle of Allah set off, he combined the noon and the afternoon prayers. If he set off before the sun had passed the midpoint of the sky, he delayed the noon prayer until he halted for the afternoon prayer. He acted similarly for the sunset prayer. If the sun set before he moved off, he combined the sunset and the night prayers, but if he moved off before sunset, he delayed the sunset prayer until he halted for the night prayer and then combined them."

Jabir ibn Abdullah said: "The Messenger of Allah,

peace be upon him, stayed at Tabuk for twenty days. He shortened the prayer (during his stay)."

If you intend to stay at a place long enough to pray twenty prayers, you must do the full prayer. Sometimes you may not intend to stay at a place for long enough to have to do the full prayer, but end up delaying your departure. In this case you must still shorten your prayers, as long as it is your intention to leave.

Tabuk

Eventually the Prophet reached Tabuk, may Allah bless him and grant him peace. The expedition took place in extreme heat. It is said that a delegation from the Byzantine Emperor came to Tabuk and that the Messenger sent them back with a reply to their king.

Then he sent out many small raiding parties. He put Khalid ibn al-Walid in charge of four hundred and twenty horsemen. Khalid fought against a man called Ukaydir at a place called Dumat al-Jandal.

Ukaydir was a Christian and a chief of his people. The two sides met in battle and Khalid captured Ukaydir. He made a treaty with him and insisted that he surrender Dumat al-Jandal. Then he made the terms of the treaty that Ukaydir should pay two thousand camels, eight hundred cattle, four hundred coats of mail and four hundred spears. A fifth of that was set aside for Allah and His Messenger. The warriors then shared out the rest.

Ukaydir was taken to the Messenger of Allah, peace be upon him, and he made peace with him. He wrote a contract of peace and Ukaydir agreed to pay the Jizyah. That is a tax that the People of the Book, such as the Christians and the Jews, pay when they do not accept Islam but agree to live under the rule of the Muslims.

Later Ukaydir accepted Islam, and with Khalid he pulled down the Christian idols and images. At that time the Prophet, peace be upon him, wrote him a new letter with a new agreement.

And what of Ka'b who had stayed behind in Madinah? He said, "The Messenger of Allah did not remember me until he reached Tabuk. While he was sitting amongst the people in Tabuk, he said, 'What has Ka'b done?' A man from Banu Salamah said, 'Messenger of Allah! He has been stopped by his two cloaks and his looking at his own flanks with pride.' Mu'adh ibn Jabal said, 'What a bad thing you have said! By Allah! Messenger of Allah! We know nothing about him but good.' The Messenger of Allah kept silent."

Aila

There is a place just at the top of the Red Sea near 'Aqabah which today is called Eilat. At that time it was called Aila. The King of Aila was also, like Ukaydir, a Christian. He had seen what had happened to Ukaydir and was afraid that the same might happen to him, so he decided to make peace before there could be any fighting. He sent a white mule as a present and a sheet for the Prophet to wear, and wrote to the Prophet that his people would stay in their place and that they would also pay the Jizyah.

In this way the army spent twenty days around Tabuk.

The Return to Madinah

Then the Prophet said, "I want to reach Madinah quickly, and whoever among you wants to accompany me, should hurry up."

When the Prophet, may Allah bless him and grant him peace, saw Madinah he said, "This is Taba." And when he saw the mountain of Uhud, he said, "This mountain loves us and we love it. Shall I tell you of the best amongst the Ansar?" They said, "Yes." He said, "The family of Bani an-Najjar, and then the family of Bani Sa'ida or Bani al-Harith ibn al-Khazraj. (The above-mentioned are the best) but there is goodness in all the families of the Ansar."

Ka'b said, "When I heard that he, peace be upon him, was on his way back to Madinah I became worried and began to think of false excuses. I said to myself, 'How can I avoid his anger tomorrow?' I took the advice of a wise member of my family in this matter, but when they said that the Messenger of Allah had come near, all the evil false excuses left my mind. I knew well that I could never get out of my situation by lying, so I decided to speak the truth."

Ka'b ibn Malik's Battle for the Truth

The Messenger of Allah arrived in the morning. Whenever he returned from a journey, he used to visit the mosque first of all and pray two rak'ahs. Then he would sit to meet the people.

When he had done all that this time, those who had failed to join the expedition came. They started offering excuses and swearing oaths before him. There were over eighty men. The Messenger of Allah accepted their excuses. He took their pledge of allegiance and asked for Allah's forgiveness for them, and left Allah as the judge of their hearts' secrets.

Then I came to him. When I greeted him, he smiled the smile of an angry person and said, "Come here." So I came and sat before him. He asked me, "What stopped you from joining us? Did you not buy an animal to carry you?"

I answered, "Yes, Messenger of Allah. By Allah, if I were sitting before anyone else in the whole world other than you, I would have avoided his anger with an excuse. By Allah, I have been given the power of speaking fluently and eloquently. By Allah, I know very well that if I tell you a lie today to seek your favour, Allah will certainly make you angry with me in the near future. But if I tell you the truth, even though you will get angry because of it, I hope for Allah's forgiveness. Really, by Allah, there was no excuse for me. By Allah, I had never been stronger or wealthier than I was when I remained behind."

Then the Messenger of Allah said, "As regards this man, he has certainly told the truth. So go away while Allah decides your case." I went out, and many men of Banu Salamah followed me saying, "By Allah, we never saw you doing any wrong action before this. Surely, you made a mistake by not offering an excuse to the Messenger of Allah as the others did who did not join him. The prayer of the Messenger of Allah to ask Allah to forgive you would have been enough for you." By Allah, they continued criticising me so much that I almost intended to return to the Prophet and accuse myself of having told a lie. Instead I asked them, "Is there anybody else who has met the same fate as I have?"

They replied, "Yes, there are two men who have said the same thing as you, and both of them were told the same as you." I said, "Who are they?" They said, "Murarah ibn ar-Rabi' al-Amri and Hilal ibn Umayyah al-Waqifi." They mentioned two excellent men who had both taken part in the battle of Badr. They were both good examples for me, so I did not change my mind when they mentioned them to me.

The Messenger of Allah, may Allah bless him and grant him peace, forbade all the Muslims to talk to the three of us, out of all those who had remained behind from that expedition. We kept away from the people. They changed their attitude towards us so much that the very land where I lived appeared strange to me as if I did not know it.

We continued in that state for fifty nights. As regards my two fellows, they remained in their houses and kept on weeping. But I was the youngest of them and the firmest. I used to go out and do the prayers along with the Muslims and roam about in the markets but no one would talk to me. I would come to the Messenger of Allah and greet him while he was sitting in his gathering after the prayer. I would wonder whether the Prophet moved his lips returning my greetings or not. I would offer my prayer near to him and look at him stealthily. When I was busy with my prayer, he would turn his face towards me. When I turned my face to him, he would turn his face away from me.

When this harsh attitude of the people had lasted for a long time, I went and climbed the wall around the garden of Abu Qatadah. He was my cousin and the person who was dearest to me. I greeted him. By Allah, he did not return my greetings. I said, "Abu Qatadah! I beg you by Allah! Don't you know that I love Allah and His Messenger?" He kept quiet. I asked him again, begging him by Allah, but he kept silent. Then I asked him again in the name of Allah. He said, "Allah and His Messenger know best." My eyes flowed with tears and I returned and jumped back over the wall.

One day, while I was walking in the market of Madinah, I saw a Christian farmer from the Nabateans of Syria. He had come to sell his grains in Madinah. He was saying, "Who will take me to Ka'b bin Malik?" The people pointed me out to him. He came and gave me a letter from the king of Ghassan in which the following was written:

> "I have been told that your friend (i.e. the Prophet) has treated you harshly. Allah will not allow you to live in a place where you feel inferior and your rights are lost. Join us, and we will console you."

(It is not unlikely for the king of Ghassan to have written to Ka'b. Remember that Ka'b was one of the two great poets of Madinah and poets were some of the most important people at that time.)

When I read it, I said to myself, "This is also a sort of test." I took the letter to the oven and made a fire with it.

When forty of the fifty nights had passed, a man came from the Messenger of Allah and said, "The Messenger of Allah orders you to keep away from your wife." I said, "Should I divorce her or what should I do?" He said, "No, only keep away from her and do not go to bed with her." The Prophet, may Allah bless him and grant him peace, sent the same message to my two fellows. Then I said to my wife, "Go to your parents and stay with them until Allah gives His decision in this matter."

The wife of Hilal ibn Umayyah came to the Messenger, peace be upon him, and said, "Messenger of Allah! Hilal ibn Umayyah is a helpless old man who has no slave to look after him. Would you dislike it if I served him?" He said, "No (you can serve him) but he should not come near you." She said, "By Allah, he has no desire for anything. By, Allah, he hasn't stopped crying since this began until this day."

Some of my family asked me, "Will you also ask the Messenger of Allah to allow your wife to serve you as he has allowed the wife of Hilal ibn Umayyah to look after him?" I said, "By Allah, I will not ask the permission of the Messenger of Allah regarding her. I do not know what the Messenger of Allah would say if I asked him to allow her to serve me while I am a young man."

I continued in that state for ten more nights after that. Then it was fifty nights from the time when the Messenger of Allah had forbidden the people to talk to us.

I prayed the morning prayer on the fiftieth morning on the roof of one of our houses. While I was sitting I was in the condition which Allah describes in the Qur'an: my own self seemed tight and narrow to me, and even the earth seemed narrow to me for all its spaciousness. Then I heard the voice of one who had climbed up the hill of Sala' calling out with his loudest voice, "Ka'b ibn Malik! Rejoice!" I fell in prostration to Allah, realising that relief had come. The Messenger of Allah had announced that Allah had accepted our repentance after the morning prayer.

People came to congratulate us. Some went to my two fellows to bring them the good news. A horseman came to me in a great hurry, but a man of Banu Aslam ran and climbed the hill. His voice was faster than the horse. When the one whose voice I had heard, came to me to give me the good news, I took off my outer clothes and dressed him with them. By Allah, I owned no other clothes than them on that day. Then I borrowed two garments and dressed in them and went to the Messenger of Allah, may Allah bless him and grant him peace.

The people started welcoming me in groups, congratulating me on Allah's accepting my repentance. They said, "Congratulations on Allah's accepting your repentance."

When I entered the mosque, I saw the Messenger of Allah sitting with people around him. Talhah ibn 'Ubaidillah quickly came to me, shook hands with me and congratulated me. By Allah, none of the Muhajirun except him got up for me. I will never forget this of Talhah.

When I greeted the Messenger of Allah his face was bright with joy. He said, "Rejoice in the best day that you have ever received since your mother gave birth to you." I said to the Prophet, may Allah bless him and grant him peace, "Is this forgiveness from you or from Allah?" He said, "No, it is from Allah." Whenever the Messenger of Allah, peace be upon him, became happy his face would shine as if it were a piece of the moon. We all knew that characteristic of him.

When I sat before him, I said, "Messenger of Allah! Because of the acceptance of my repentance, I give up all my wealth as sadaqah for the sake of Allah and His Messenger." The Messenger of Allah said, "Keep some of your wealth. It will be better for you." I said, "I will keep my share from Khaybar," and added, "Messenger of Allah! Allah has saved me because I told the truth; so it is a part of my repentance that I will only tell the truth as long as I am alive."

By Allah, I do not know any Muslim whom Allah has helped more for telling the truth than me. Since I told the truth to the Messenger of Allah until today, I have never intended to tell a lie. I hope that Allah will also save me from telling lies for the rest of my life.

Allah revealed to His Messenger the ayat:

> "Truly, Allah has turned towards the Prophet, and the Emigrants and the Helpers, those who followed him in the hour of difficulty, after the hearts of a group of them almost deviated. Then He turned towards them. Truly, He is All-Pitying, All-Merciful to them," up until His words, "O who you believe! Fear Allah and be with the truthful ones." (Qur'an, Surat at-Tawbah: 117-119)

By Allah, Allah has never given me, apart from His guiding me to Islam, any greater blessing than the fact that I did not tell a lie to the Messenger of Allah. That would have destroyed me as it destroyed those who told lies. Allah describes those who told lies in the worst way He ever described anybody. Allah said:

"They (the hypocrites) will swear to you by Allah when you return to them, so that you turn away from them. So turn away from them! They are dirty. Their shelter will be Jahannam as repayment for what they earned. They will swear to you to make you pleased with them, but even if you are pleased with them, truly Allah is not pleased with degenerate people." (Qur'an, Surat at-Tawbah: 95-96)

Ka'b added, "We three were completely different from the ones whose excuses the Messenger of Allah accepted when they swore oaths to him. He took their pledge of allegiance and asked Allah to forgive them. But the Messenger of Allah left our case pending until Allah gave His judgement about it.

Allah says about that:

"And (Allah turned) to the three who were left behind, so that when the earth became narrow for them, for all its spaciousness, and their own selves became constricted for them and they realised that there was no refuge from Allah except in Him, He turned to them so that they would turn to Him. Allah is the Ever-Returning, the All-Merciful." (Qur'an, Surat at-Tawbah: 118)

That which Allah says in this ayah – "the three who were left behind" – is not about our failure to take part in the expedition. It refers to the Prophet's delaying making a decision about our case. That is in contrast to the case of those who swore oaths to him. He excused them by accepting their excuses.

The Hypocrites

Ka'b told the truth, but the hypocrites lied. They were not punished in this world for their lying, but Allah tells us that they will be in the lowest levels of the Fire in the next life.

On another occasion, the hypocrites slandered A'ishah, may Allah be pleased with her. Some of the Muslims heard the rumour. They were not very thoughtful and they repeated it to others.

Then Allah revealed that A'ishah was innocent, and He revealed that people who slander believing women must be punished. The hypocrites again swore an oath that they had said nothing bad about her, and so they were not punished. The Muslims who had repeated the story were honest and admitted it. They were punished.

Lying is a terrible thing. The writer George Bernard Shaw once said that one of the problems with lying is not that other people do not believe you, but that you stop believing yourself.

The Last Battle

That was the last expedition to battle in which the Prophet, may Allah bless him and grant him peace, took part. However, his last command to an army was when he placed Usamah in charge of another great force also to march against the Byzantines. Usamah was twenty years old. It was his father, Zaid, who had died leading the Muslims against the Byzantines in Mu'tah some years before.

This struggle that Sayyiduna Muhammad, peace be upon him, began against the Byzantine Empire continued after him. The Companions cut the Empire in half within a few years. A non-Muslim writer says that there were three reasons which helped the Muslims to win.

First, the Byzantines persecuted other Christians who had different beliefs and practices from their own, whereas the Muslims accepted all the Christian groups as being Christians and did not interfere in their affairs.

Second, the Byzantines taxed people very heavily, but the Muslims only charged the Jizyah and a tax on the land. The Muslim taxes were much lighter and easier than the Byzantine taxes.

Third, when people accepted Islam, they had no taxes to pay at all accept the zakat, which is an act of worship for Allah, and which is given to the poor and the needy. When the Christians heard all this, they did not really want to fight against Islam, and so the Muslims won much more easily than they would have otherwise.

For centuries the Muslims tried to capture Constantinople. Constantine had rebuilt the old Greek city of Byzantium with enormous thick walls in 328 CE. The Muslims first laid siege to it in 677 CE, under the command of the khalifah Mu'awiyyah, may Allah be pleased with him.

There, under the walls of the city, the Companion Abu Ayyub al-Ansari died, may Allah be pleased with him. He was the man with whom the Messenger, peace be upon him, had first stayed when he emigrated to Madinah. Abu Ayyub is buried there in Istanbul where today his grave is visited by Muslims from all over the world.

Not all of the Muslim rulers continued the jihad, but when the Ottomans appeared in what is today called Turkey, they insisted on carrying on the da'wah and the jihad. They opened a lot of the old Byzantine Empire, much of which was in Europe.

Finally, the Ottomans opened the city of Constantinople to Islam in 1453 CE. It had taken almost 800 years. They renamed it 'Istanbul'.

But remember that the original Roman Empire had split into two: the Western Roman Empire and the Eastern. The Ottomans opened the Eastern half, and then they focused on trying to open the Western half. They were unable to do that, although they did come right into Western Europe. They even laid siege to Vienna at one point.

This Last Battle for the truth of Islam is not over. It must begin again as Islam always begins by inviting non-Muslims to clear knowledge of the unity of Allah and the messengership of Muhammad, may Allah bless him and grant him peace.